THE MANSON FAMILY MURDERS

By Tom Streissguth

CONTENT CONSULTANT

Claudia Verhoeven
Associate Professor, History
Cornell University

AMERICAN
CRIME
STORIES

Essential Library

An Imprint of Abdo Publishing | abdobooks.com

ABDOBOOKS.COM

Published by Abdo Publishing, a division of ABDO, PO Box 398166, Minneapolis, Minnesota 55439. Copyright © 2020 by Abdo Consulting Group, Inc. International copyrights reserved in all countries. No part of this book may be reproduced in any form without written permission from the publisher. Essential Library™ is a trademark and logo of Abdo Publishing.

Printed in the United States of America, North Mankato, Minnesota.
092019
012020

THIS BOOK CONTAINS RECYCLED MATERIALS

SEP 0 5 2020

Cover Photo: AP Images
Interior Photos: Reed Saxon/AP Images, 5; Frank Tewkesbury/AP Images, 8; AP Images, 11, 15, 24–25, 29, 36–37, 41, 53, 56, 71, 74, 81, 87, 90–91, 96; iStockphoto, 17; 1542980Globe Photos/MediaPunch/MediaPunch/Ipx/AP Images, 21; Ralph Crane/The LIFE Picture Collection/Getty Images, 27, 62–63; Robert W. Klein/AP Images, 32; George Birch/AP Images, 34; Rainer Lesniewski/iStockphoto, 38; David F. Smith/AP Images, 47, 77; Michael Ochs Archives/Getty Images, 50; Gary Kazanjian/AP Images, 66; Albert Foster/Mirrorpix/Getty Images, 68; Matt Terhune/Splash News/Newscom, 72; Wally Fong/AP Images, 85

Editor: Charly Haley
Series Designer: Melissa Martin

LIBRARY OF CONGRESS CONTROL NUMBER: 2019941968

PUBLISHER'S CATALOGING-IN-PUBLICATION DATA

Names: Streissguth, Tom, author.
Title: The Manson family murders / by Tom Streissguth
Description: Minneapolis, Minnesota: Abdo Publishing, 2020 | Series: American crime stories | Includes online resources and index.
Identifiers: ISBN 9781532190117 (lib. bdg) | ISBN 9781532175961 (ebook)
Subjects: LCSH: Manson, Charles, 1934-2017--Juvenile literature. | Mass murder investigation--Juvenile literature. | Cults--Juvenile literature. | Trials (Murder)--California--Juvenile literature. | Homicide--Juvenile literature.
Classification: DDC 364.152--dc23

CONTENTS

CHAPTER ONE
MURDER ON CIELO DRIVE
4

CHAPTER TWO
TWO HOMICIDE CASES
14

CHAPTER THREE
CHARLES MANSON
26

CHAPTER FOUR
TURNING TO MURDER
36

CHAPTER FIVE
HELTER SKELTER
52

CHAPTER SIX
CLOSING IN ON THE FAMILY
62

CHAPTER SEVEN
MAKING THE CASE
70

CHAPTER EIGHT
THE TRIAL
80

CHAPTER NINE
THE VERDICTS
90

Timeline   98
Essential Facts   100
Glossary   102
Additional Resources   104

Source Notes   106
Index   110
About the Author   112

CHAPTER ONE

MURDER ON CIELO DRIVE

t was a warm summer morning in Los Angeles, California, on August 9, 1969. Winifred Chapman was running late. Chapman had a good job and didn't want any trouble. She worked as a housekeeper in a mansion in Benedict Canyon, at the end of winding Cielo Drive. Hidden from the road by trees and protected by an electronic gate, the mansion at 10050 Cielo Drive had a sparkling pool, a well-kept lawn, a guesthouse, and great views of the city. Like many of the houses in this neighborhood, it had been a home for movie stars, music producers, and other wealthy Angelenos.

The mansion was a nice place for Chapman to work. But as usual, her bus was behind schedule. The bus finally stopped at the foot of Benedict Canyon. Chapman would normally walk the rest of the way, but she spotted an acquaintance with a car. She caught a ride into the dry scrub hills, got off in front of the

The mansion at 10050 Cielo Drive, shown here in 1992, was demolished in 1994.

house, and made her way through the gate. There were some strange cars parked in the driveway, but that was nothing out of the ordinary. The home's residents often had visitors.

The Discovery

Chapman walked to a door near the kitchen and dining room. This was not the mansion's main entrance. Chapman unlocked the door and stepped inside. The house was quiet, but it was still early in the day, and this house always felt somewhat serene. Actress Candice Bergen, who lived there for a while, once said, "There was a cartoonlike perfection about it. You waited to find Bambi drinking from the pool, Thumper dozing in the flowers, to hear the dwarfs whistling home at the end of the day. It was a fairy-tale place . . . where nothing could go wrong."[1]

Chapman walked through the dining room toward the main living room at the center of the house. It was a long room with a low, beamed ceiling and a stone fireplace. As Chapman walked into the room, she saw a dead body.

Chapman screamed. She felt a wave of confusion, terror, and panic. The serene house had become a place of horror. Chapman saw blood on the walls. On the front door, someone had written the word *Pig* in blood.

Chapman ran out of the house and toward the driveway. She saw another body in one of the cars near the front gate.

She rushed to the nearest neighboring house and pounded on the door. "Murder, death, bodies, blood!" she wailed.[2] There was no answer.

Police Arrive

Chapman ran to the next house, at 10090 Cielo Drive, where Ray Asin and his son were preparing to go out. The Asins tried to calm her. Chapman led them back to 10050, where they looked in at the gate and stopped. Ray Asin returned home to call the police. On the third try, he finally got through.

First on the scene, Officer Jerry DeRosa parked his squad car in front of the Asins' house, where Chapman and the Asins were waiting. Trembling and nervous, Chapman wasn't much help in preparing DeRosa for what he would find.

DeRosa walked through the gate at the end of Cielo Drive and into the house at 10050. In the living room, actress Sharon Tate was dead. She was lying on her side, in front of the

SHARON TATE

Sharon Tate had struggled for several years to become successful as an actress in Hollywood. She had played small roles in a few television series, including *The Beverly Hillbillies*, and in several movies, including *Barabbas*, *Eye of the Devil*, and *The Fearless Vampire Killers*, a film directed by her future husband, Roman Polanski. After Tate was killed, several of these movies were rereleased to packed theaters in Los Angeles and around the country. Getting top billing on the marquees for these features, for the first time in her career, was Sharon Tate.

Actress Sharon Tate was 26 years old when she was murdered in her home.

couch, with her right arm up around her head. A few feet away, well-known men's hairstylist Jay Sebring was also lying on his side, dead. The two were tied together by a rope that had been flung across a ceiling beam. There was a lot of blood on the carpet.

Asin and Chapman told police the little information they knew: the house was owned by a Hollywood agent named Rudi Altobelli, but he was renting it to Tate and her husband, movie director Roman Polanski. Tate was pregnant with their son when she was killed. Polanski was in London, England, at the time of the murders.

A caretaker lived in a guesthouse on the property. Two other people also lived in the main house: Abigail Folger, daughter of the coffee tycoon Peter Folger, and her boyfriend, Voytek Frykowski. Among the cars in the driveway that day was a black Porsche that Chapman had seen before. It belonged to Sebring.

Outside, just as DeRosa spotted the slumped-over body in the car parked near the gate, Officer William Whisenhunt arrived. The two men walked toward the house with their guns drawn. They found two more bodies on the lawn, which were later identified as Folger and Frykowski.

More police soon arrived on the scene. They began to gather whatever evidence they could find. They found horn-rimmed glasses and a broken gun grip on the floor. A knife was found stuffed into the cushion of a chair.

Two officers left the main house and proceeded past the pool to the guesthouse. In the cottage, they found William

ROMAN POLANSKI

During the 1960s, two of Roman Polanski's films, *Repulsion* and *Cul-de-Sac*, won awards at the Berlin International Film Festival. After meeting and marrying Sharon Tate, he made *Rosemary's Baby* in 1968. His film *Chinatown* was nominated for best picture and won the Oscar for best screenplay of 1974. Polanski moved back to Europe after the murder of his wife, but he often traveled to the United States to work on his film projects. In 1977, Polanski was criminally charged with having sex with a minor. He fled the United States before his trial concluded and has remained outside of the country ever since. He could be sentenced to prison if he returns.

Garretson, the property's caretaker, asleep on a couch. They dragged Garretson outside and pushed him down on the lawn. "What's wrong?" Garretson asked, over and over. "Shut up," barked one of the officers. "We'll show you."[3]

The officers pulled Garretson to his feet and then walked with him to the main house. Garretson saw the bodies on the lawn, but the police kept him out of the living room. Under questioning, Garretson described his evening. He had been up late, listening to music. Steve Parent, a friend, had come to visit. Garretson said Parent left the guesthouse at about midnight. Parent was the man found dead in his car at the gate. The police arrested Garretson on suspicion of murder in relation to all five deaths.

Reporters and photographers soon arrived at the mansion. The stream of police calls to Cielo Drive was picked up by newspaper reporters, who monitor police scanners for crimes, accidents, and other newsworthy events. A busy scene unfolded as police, reporters, and onlookers struggled to understand what had happened. How were five people brutally killed overnight at this quiet mansion?

The Story Breaks

Los Angeles Times reporter Dial Torgerson began his story with a straightforward synopsis: "Film star Sharon Tate, another woman and three men were found slain Saturday, their bodies

THE VICTIMS
AT CIELO DRIVE

SHARON TATE, 26

Actress, known for *Valley of the Dolls* (1967)
and *The Wrecking Crew* (1968)

JAY SEBRING, 35

Famous men's hairstylist

ABIGAIL FOLGER, 25

Daughter of famous coffee
company owner Peter Folger

VOYTEK FRYKOWSKI, 32

Actor

STEVE PARENT, 18

High school graduate, soon-to-be
college student

These five people were murdered at a mansion at 10050 Cielo Drive,
Los Angeles, California, on August 9, 1969.

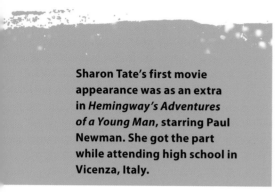

Sharon Tate's first movie appearance was as an extra in *Hemingway's Adventures of a Young Man*, starring Paul Newman. She got the part while attending high school in Vicenza, Italy.

scattered around a Benedict Canyon estate in what police said resembled a ritualistic mass murder."[4] The story, on page one of Sunday's *Times*, ran beside a photograph of a smiling Sharon Tate.

The news story sent Los Angeles into shock. Fearful for their lives, the residents of Benedict Canyon, friends and acquaintances of the victims, and essentially everyone in the city's vast movie industry began taking precautions. They believed merciless "ritualistic" killers were on the loose. It seemed anyone could be the next victim.

At the Cielo Drive mansion, forensics technicians had spent most of August 9 taking blood samples and examining furniture, walls, and doors for fingerprints. It was a challenging task. The evidence of chaotic violence in and around the house prompted the police to call the Los Angeles County coroner, Dr. Thomas Noguchi, directly to the scene.

The work of police and forensics was not always thorough. Joe Granado, with the Scientific Investigation Division of the Los Angeles Police Department (LAPD), took dozens of blood samples but found it impossible to include every stain of blood. DeRosa, while leaving the property, pushed a button to open the electronic front gate—and, in doing so, smudged an important fingerprint. When asked later why he left the scene, a shaken DeRosa replied, "I had to get out of there."[5]

Although DeRosa and other police officers were accustomed to working with murder and death, the gruesome scene at Cielo Drive still shook them. For the LAPD, this would be a long and tough investigation. There were five dead, and the entire city was on alert, frightened. Newspapers and television stations across the country were speculating and demanding answers. It was the kind of situation a police department dreads—and it was about to get worse. This mass murder was just part of a series of violent killings yet to come.

THE MANSION'S OWNER

As the owner of 10050 Cielo Drive, Rudi Altobelli was disturbed by the crime that happened on his property. But he soon moved back into the house anyway, finding it difficult to rent it after the murders. Altobelli dealt with the crime by asking for compensation. He sent a bill to the Tate family for the cleanup expenses. Then, he sued Sharon Tate's estate, claiming she had not bought liability insurance as required by the lease and that the murders had damaged the value of his house. He also sued for Tate allowing Folger and Frykowski to use the house as a residence. Although his demand was for more than $400,000, the court system was not sympathetic, eventually awarding him just $4,350 in damages.[6]

TWO
HOMICIDE CASES

Late in the evening of August 10—less than 48 hours after Winifred Chapman had made her grisly discovery at 10050 Cielo Drive—Frank Struthers, the 15-year-old son of Rosemary LaBianca, arrived at her home at 3301 Waverly Drive, Los Angeles. Frank's mother had remarried, making Frank the stepson of Leno LaBianca, who owned Gateway Ranch Markets, a chain of grocery stores. The LaBiancas lived in a big white house in the Los Feliz neighborhood.

Frank sensed something was wrong that night. Strangely, Leno LaBianca had left his boat hooked to his car in the driveway. Frank also found the window shades drawn and the home silent. Frank thought the LaBiancas must have been home, but there was no answer to his knock on the door.

The LaBianca house

Worried, Frank walked several blocks to a pay phone and called his sister. Suzan Struthers soon arrived at the house with her boyfriend, Joe Dorgan. The three found a house key in Rosemary LaBianca's car. After entering through the back door, Frank and Joe walked through the house while Suzan remained in the kitchen.

In the living room, they discovered the body of Leno LaBianca. He had been brutally stabbed to death and was lying on the floor with a pillowcase around his head, tied up with a lamp cord. Frank and Joe rushed back to the kitchen. Standing there, waiting, Suzan had spotted something scrawled on the refrigerator door. It looked like it was written in blood.

The three left the house and ran to a neighbor, who called the police. Sergeant Danny Galindo, a homicide detective who had been assigned to the Tate case, arrived at the LaBianca residence at approximately 1:00 a.m. Police quickly discovered the body of Rosemary LaBianca in a bedroom. She also had a pillowcase around her head and was tied up like her husband. The couple had been dead for several hours.

There was writing in blood all over the house. *Death to Pigs* was scrawled on the walls of the living room. Near the front door was the word *Rise*. On the refrigerator door were the words *Healter Skelter*, with a misspelling of *Helter*.

The Investigations

While the Los Angeles County Sheriff's Department was investigating the murders at the Tate residence, the LaBianca case was assigned to the robbery-homicide division of the Los Angeles Police Department. At first, the two departments did not make any connection between the two crimes.

Investigators soon concluded that the motive of the LaBianca murders was not robbery. While searching Leno LaBianca's car, detectives had found his wallet with cash and credit cards. Inside the house, they also found jewelry, watches, collectible coins, weapons, and camera equipment. All of these items could have been easily sold for cash. Why leave them? Why write nonsensical phrases in blood on the walls and in

The LaBianca house was about 10 miles (16 km) east of the Tate house.

THE CRIME SCENES

The Tate House
0050 Cielo Drive

The LaBianca House
3301 Waverly Drive

the kitchen? What could the motive possibly be for savagely murdering these people in their home?

For experienced homicide detectives, nothing was routine at these crime scenes. None of the victims had known criminal associations, although illegal drugs were found at the Tate residence. The victims were not involved in any known family, business, or legal disputes. Despite all of the physical evidence—the blood, the weapons at the scenes—there were few leads on the identity of the killer or killers. At first, investigators worked on the theories that a drug deal had led to the mass murder at Cielo Drive and that some kind of alleged organized crime connection had resulted in the LaBianca murders. However, these theories were later disproven.

With few facts and little information offered by the police, the media speculated on motives. These included widespread speculation that the Tate murder had occurred as either a wild drug-infused party that went horribly wrong or some kind of bloody satanic ritual. Polanski's work on horror movies also provided fodder for the ritual murder theory.

Questions for a Witness

For a couple of days, William Garretson was the prime suspect in the Tate slayings. He had been hired to be the mansion's live-in caretaker by Rudi Altobelli, the owner of the property. Garretson was a teenager just out of high school who had recently moved to Los Angeles from Lancaster, Ohio. He had no criminal background and, as far as detectives could tell, no motive.

But Garretson had no alibi for that night, as his visiting friend was dead; he lived alone, and he hadn't left the property on the night of the murders. Police were also curious about why Garretson had not heard anything that night while others much farther from the Tate residence had heard screams and gunshots.

The day after the Tate murders, Garretson was given a polygraph test, which he passed. His explanation for not hearing anything—that he was listening to music at the time—was accepted by the police, who examined the volume controls on Garretson's stereo and ran sound tests in the front yard, where Folger and Frykowski were killed. Still in custody on the day of the LaBianca murders, Garretson was dismissed as a suspect and released on August 11, the following day.

WILLIAM GARRETSON

After being ruled out as a suspect for the murders, William Garretson returned home to Lancaster, Ohio. He stayed in Ohio for the rest of his life. Newspaper reporters and other people often asked him about his experience on the night of the murders. He also received several lucrative offers to tell his story in a book, but he never accepted them.

Clearing Garretson of the crime meant the killers were still on the loose. Fear spread across Los Angeles. Sales of weapons, guard dogs, and strong door locks skyrocketed. The murders had happened during a particularly deadly weekend in Los Angeles—28 homicides were recorded in the city just over that weekend, more than 10 times the normal rate.[1] People wondered how many of these might have been random killings committed by ritualistic murderers.

Speculation about the motives and the killers' identities was rampant, as were lurid notions of wild parties and strange rituals at 10050 Cielo Drive. Two weeks after the murders, a *Newsweek* magazine article said, "Some suspect that the group was amusing itself with some sort of black magic rites as well as drugs that night. . . . Indeed, a group of friends speculates that the murders resulted from a brutal mock execution that got out of hand."[2]

Roman Polanski

Soon after his wife was killed, Polanski returned to Los Angeles from London. Traumatized by the murders, he decided to give Sharon Tate's car and personal belongings to her parents. Polanski got rid of other possessions that reminded him of his late wife, too. These included clothes, jewelry, and the baby bassinet she had recently bought for the son they were expecting.

Polanski, *left*, and Tate had been married for about a year before Tate was murdered.

What made it most difficult for Polanski were the accusations of wild parties going on at the Cielo Drive house. The rumors of drug deals, satanic rituals, and general rowdiness were a lie, according to family, friends, and anyone who knew Tate. Under questioning by police, Polanski said Tate "was so sweet and lovely that I didn't believe it, you know. I'd had bad experiences and I didn't believe that people like that existed."[3]

But Polanski could provide no clues to who his wife's killers might be, and, like everyone else, he was speculating on a possible motive. Was he the real target of the crime? "It could be some type of witchcraft," he told the police. "A maniac or something. This execution, this tragedy, indicates to me it must be some kind of nut, you know. I wouldn't be surprised if I were the target."[4]

Ruling Out a Connection

There were several similarities between the Tate and LaBianca murders. Both involved multiple stabbings. A large buck knife or bayonet had been used by the killers. At both scenes, the victims had been tied up and words were written in blood on walls and doors. The writing included *Death to Pigs* at the LaBianca house and *Pig* on the front door of the Tate house.

Nevertheless, after weeks of investigation, the LAPD announced in late August that it had officially ruled out any connection between the Tate and LaBianca murders. The crime locations were far apart; there was no link between the victims; and a possible drug motive to both murders was out, as no drugs were found at the LaBianca residence. LAPD inspector K. J. McCauley told reporters, "I don't see any connection between this murder and

LIFE AND DEATH OF A HOUSE

The house at 10050 Cielo Drive was built in the 1940s for French actress Michele Morgan. After the murders in 1969, owner Rudi Altobelli lived in the house for 20 years until he was able to rent it again. The last resident of the house was Trent Reznor of the rock group Nine Inch Nails. The dark history of the place appealed to Reznor, who filmed one of his band's music videos at the residence. But after being confronted by Sharon Tate's sister, Reznor had a change of heart and soon moved out. Altobelli had the house torn down in 1994. Then he built a larger home on the property and had the address changed to 10066 Cielo Drive.

Police investigate the crime scene at Tate's house.

the others. They're too widely removed. I just don't see any connection."[5]

The distance between the murder scenes also meant they were each handled by different law enforcement jurisdictions—the county and the city of Los Angeles. As a result, detectives failed to coordinate their investigations. Until a few suspects were arrested much later, the Tate and LaBianca murders were treated officially as unconnected crimes.

In the meantime, life went on in Los Angeles. People went shopping, took their dogs for walks, and went to work. In early September, a reward of $25,000 was announced by several well-known people in the film industry, including actors Peter Sellers and Warren Beatty, who were friends of Tate and Polanski. There were hundreds of anonymous tips, which the police dutifully investigated, but none proved useful in solving the case.

CHAPTER THREE

CHARLES MANSON

Kicking up big clouds of dust, police cars and motorcycles roared up the highways that crossed the dry ridges and gullies north of Los Angeles. It was August 16, 1969, just one week after the Tate murders. The police were headed toward an abandoned movie set known as Spahn Ranch. They knew whom to expect at the property: the owner, 80-year-old George Spahn, some of his helpers, and a group of suspected auto thieves.

Two police helicopters rumbled overhead as officers sped onto Spahn's property. In the ramshackle cabins and stables of Spahn Ranch, panic spread, and people began to scatter. There were plenty of places to hide. The ranch was made up to look like an old Western town, set in a maze of rocky, sagebrush-covered hills.

The road to Spahn Ranch

For several weeks, Los Angeles County sheriff's deputy William Gleason had been investigating the ranch. Neighbors had been complaining about noise and parties, and police and firefighters had responded to several calls about the ranch. The sheriff's department also had a couple of informants on the inside.

Gleason knew from one of these informants that there were plenty of weapons at the property. He suspected that an auto theft ring was operating out of the ranch, and he knew about the extensive criminal records of several people living there. At least one resident was still on parole from a long prison sentence. Parolees—who can be rearrested and held for breaking the terms of their release—are often cooperative with police, which can help in identifying suspects or gathering other information.

Gleason's investigation gave the sheriff's department probable cause for the August 16 raid on Spahn Ranch. Dashing from their vehicles, police rushed into the buildings, rounding up and arresting people on suspicion of auto theft. By the time the raid was over, the officers had gathered 26 adults and five children. One of the suspects—a short, long-haired, scraggly-looking man—was identified as the group's leader. His name was Charles Manson.

Charles Manson, 1969

A Life of Crime

In his autobiography, published in 1986, Manson described the start of his life. "On November 12, 1934, while living in Cincinnati, Ohio, unwed and only sixteen, my mother gave birth to a son. Hospital records list the child as 'no name Maddox.' The child—me, Charles Milles Manson—was an outlaw from birth."[1]

William Manson left only his name behind when he left Kathleen Maddox, to whom he was in fact legally married, and her baby son. Charles Manson had no memory of his father. His mother was a thief and an alcoholic. In 1939, she robbed a gas station in Charleston, West Virginia, which landed her in jail. Manson was five years old at the time.

With his mother in jail, young Manson went to live with his grandparents and later his aunt and uncle. These relatives gave him a stable home, but he couldn't stay out of trouble. Starting at age nine, he was moved in and out of juvenile reformatories. At age 13, he committed his first armed robbery.

When he wasn't in jail or a reformatory, Manson liked to move around. In 1951, he hit the road with a couple of fellow inmates after escaping from the Indiana Boys School near Indianapolis. The trio headed to California, robbing gas stations for money along the way. Later, Manson was busted for larceny and auto theft. He also fathered two sons, with two different legal wives, in the 1950s. In 1960, at the age of 26, he began serving a ten-year prison sentence after being convicted of forging a check and violating the terms of his parole.

For the next seven years, Manson lived at a maximum-security prison on McNeil Island in Washington. While there, Manson went through several evaluations as the prison staff tried to decide whether to release him on parole. One report read: "He hides his loneliness, resentment, and hostility behind a façade of superficial ingratiation. An energetic, young-appearing person whose verbalization flows quite easily, he gestures profoundly and can dramatize situations to hold the listener's attention."[2]

Even to tough prison officials who deal with convicts applying for parole on a daily basis, Manson could be a very convincing talker. In early 1967, Manson persuaded a parole

LESSONS FROM A GANGSTER

While incarcerated at McNeil Island, Manson struck up a friendship with Alvin "Creepy" Karpis, a Prohibition-era gangster who taught Manson how to play the guitar. With a lot of time on his hands, Manson began writing songs. Certain of his own musical talent, he began planning a future career as a professional singer/songwriter.

Karpis, the last survivor of the famous Ma Barker gang of bank robbers, wasn't so sure. Later interviewed about his experiences with Manson, Karpis recalled, "This kid approaches me to request music lessons. He wants to learn guitar and become a music star. Little Charlie is so lazy and shiftless, I doubt if he'll put in the time required to learn."[3]

board to grant him freedom from McNeil Island. Not long after that, he drifted down to the Haight-Ashbury neighborhood of San Francisco, California, and the Summer of Love.

Starting a Family

San Francisco had become a magnet for young people from all over the country who wanted to drop out of traditional society and live a different way. These hippies gave up conventional

Hippies sometimes gathered on the streets of Haight-Ashbury for anti-war demonstrations and other protests during the Summer of Love, 1967.

jobs and ambition. They denounced consumerism. Drugs were plentiful, and living arrangements were flexible, with many people living in communes. Haight-Ashbury, a neighborhood at the eastern end of Golden Gate Park, attracted thousands of hippies who declared the Summer of Love in 1967.

Manson saw Haight-Ashbury as a promising place to escape the attention of law enforcement. In San Francisco, he also developed a talent for winning attentive followers. He had been studying Scientology and various occult movements. He adopted and combined these ideas into a personal philosophy, delivered in a convincing and confident voice that attracted listeners.

Manson would preach for hours, and Mary Brunner heard every word. When she first met Manson, whom she called "Charlie," she was working as a librarian at the University of California, Berkeley. She was a quiet and steady person, not someone who made rash decisions. But she found Manson's words so compelling, so interesting and convincing, that she gave up her job and followed him across the San Francisco Bay to Haight-Ashbury. With this, Brunner became the first member of the Manson Family.

Several other young women followed Brunner into Manson's group. Manson preached about love and sharing. But he also taught his followers about theft. Eventually, the Family

Members of the Family were loyal to Manson, listening to his preachings and following his suggestions.

THE HOUSE IN HAIGHT-ASHBURY

In April 1967, Manson moved into a two-story stucco house in Haight-Ashbury. While living in that house, 636 Cole Street, Manson began collecting members of his Family. They included Mary Brunner, future murderer Patricia Krenwinkel, and Lynette "Squeaky" Fromme, who later, in 1975, would unsuccessfully attempt to kill President Gerald Ford in Sacramento, California.

stole cars to get around and credit cards to buy supplies. If they ran short of money, they dived into dumpsters and trash cans, searching for food.

After some time, Manson found San Francisco to be problematic. He felt there were too many distractions in the city, and several other hippie gurus were competing for followers around Haight-Ashbury. Manson had also started a band, which commanded much of his attention. He was obsessed with the Beatles, a British rock group that was immensely popular worldwide, and he was sure that his own group would be even more famous—if only he met the right people, caught a break, and could get his music out to the masses. To get his music career moving, there was only one place to go: Los Angeles. So, Manson loaded up the Family in a bus and moved down the California coast.

CHAPTER FOUR

TURNING
TO MURDER

n the late 1940s, a dairy delivery man from Pennsylvania named George Spahn joined the multitudes of people heading to California in search of sunshine and a place in, or at least close to, the glamorous Hollywood movie industry. Spahn bought a ranch in the Simi Hills north of Los Angeles. The expansive property had been used as a movie set a couple of times in the past, but under Spahn's ownership, it became known as the Spahn Movie Ranch. He promoted it as a convenient place for Hollywood directors to shoot Westerns.

The ranch had hosted filming of *Duel in the Sun* with Gregory Peck in 1946. The television Western *The Lone Ranger* shot several episodes at Spahn Ranch in the 1950s, and the 1960s TV hit *Bonanza* followed. But the Western genre of movies and

Spahn Ranch, shown in 1969, was about 20 miles (32 km) northeast of Los Angeles.

television began losing popularity in the 1960s, and the ranch soon fell into disrepair. By early 1968, Spahn was growing old and in need of ranch hands, anyone willing to help maintain the place in exchange for a place to live.

Manson jumped at the chance. The Family had been hanging around Los Angeles for several months. They lived

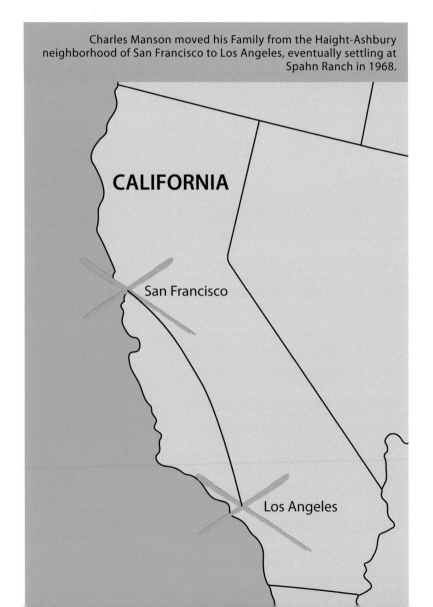

Charles Manson moved his Family from the Haight-Ashbury neighborhood of San Francisco to Los Angeles, eventually settling at Spahn Ranch in 1968.

off petty thievery and temporarily stayed in the homes of sympathetic friends including Dennis Wilson, a member of the Beach Boys, a famous band. Manson believed Spahn Ranch's remote location would make it easier for him to keep an eye on his collection of young followers. He also thought it would help him avoid the attention of the police. So, in August 1968, Manson moved his Family to the Spahn Ranch.

Growing the Family

Although the hippie counterculture that Manson had adopted preached peace and love, Manson himself often talked about a coming race war, an event he called "Helter Skelter," after the title of a Beatles song. Manson was a racist, believing that black people and white people should live separately. He also believed that racial tensions fueled by centuries of white people oppressing black people would soon erupt into the violent conflict Helter Skelter. Manson preached about the important role he believed his Family would play in Helter Skelter, saying they might even have to set off the conflict themselves. But Manson had a plan for how to survive the supposed Helter Skelter. He said the Family would take shelter somewhere until the conflict was over.

Manson also railed against possessions. In his opinion, owning things was a trap set by what he called "the Establishment," referring to American society, which he believed fixated on consumerism. He believed the purpose of the consumer society was to inspire anxiety and pump up the need to constantly shop and buy more stuff. He told his followers that they shouldn't need money and possessions— they should treasure only love, brotherhood, music, and drugs.

Manson put this idea into action by gradually taking control of his followers' cash and credit cards. Family women stole what food or other essentials they could and dived into dumpsters to collect stuff that the so-called Establishment threw away. The Family also used stolen credit cards to buy clothing and other necessities.

Manson banned his Family from having clocks, watches, and calendars.

Instead of collecting a lot of material things, the Family collected people. If they found a woman sitting alone on a curb or hitchhiking on a lonely road, they would offer a friendly ride, followed by an invitation to join the Family for a while. For some, the Family seemed as good a chance as any that life had offered. Many young women who joined the Family had problems with their parents, had run away from home, or were living alone on the streets. To outsiders, the Manson Family seemed loving and happy. Joining them meant being with a big group of friends, laughing and singing, living carefree, and basically doing whatever they wanted.

A group of Manson Family members in 1970

It was an easy decision for Dianne Lake, who met the Manson Family at a party when she was just 14. She later wrote, "There was something about this group of girls and about Charlie, and while I wasn't sure what it was, I immediately knew I wanted to be a part of it. Like a raindrop joining a puddle, I blended in easily, my loneliness disappearing. For the first time in my life, I felt like I was in the right place at the right time."[1]

Like Lake, most of the Family members were young women from middle-class families. They enjoyed Manson's attention and the feeling of a close-knit group of people looking after each other. They spent many evenings listening to Manson talk or play the guitar.

Manson had some talent for writing songs, and he tried to make connections in LA's busy music industry. He was successful in befriending Wilson, one of the Beach Boys, and had even persuaded Hollywood music producer Terry Melcher to come out to the ranch for an audition. Manson's music interest also helped him persuade Bobby Beausoleil, a talented musician and actor, to spend some time at Spahn Ranch. At age 15, Beausoleil had run away from his family in Santa Barbara and made his way to Los Angeles, then to San Francisco. While living in Haight-Ashbury, Beausoleil played with several rock bands and appeared in movies directed by filmmaker Kenneth Anger.

Beausoleil eventually moved back to Los Angeles. There, he met Manson. Manson appreciated Beausoleil's guitar skills,

TERRY MELCHER'S HOME

The Tate and LaBianca murders shook up Hollywood's entertainment industry. Seeing themselves as targets of a crazed serial killer, many people working in the industry protected their homes with security systems, weapons, and guard dogs. Among them was Terry Melcher, who had feared Manson even before the murders.

Melcher knew Manson personally and had visited Spahn Ranch to listen to him perform music. Melcher also knew that Manson had grown angry because Melcher didn't give him a record deal. When Melcher's mother, iconic actress Doris Day, heard her son talking about this strange, angry hippie guru and his Family, she urged Melcher to get away from the house he was renting, where he had first met Manson. In January 1969, Melcher moved out of the residence he had been sharing with actress Candice Bergen—at 10050 Cielo Drive.

and Beausoleil enjoyed the company of Manson's many female followers, who called him "Cupid." He also liked the Family's easy access to drugs and their nonstop partying. To Beausoleil, living with the Family felt almost like being a rock star.

While living with the Family, Beausoleil became friends with a young, soft-spoken musician named Gary Hinman. The two often hung out at Hinman's small house in Topanga Canyon, in the hills north of Malibu. Over time, Beausoleil got the impression that although Hinman lived simply, he actually had some money—perhaps from his family or from an inheritance. When that information got back to Manson, Hinman's fate was sealed.

The Murder of Gary Hinman

On July 25, 1969, three members of the Manson Family went to Hinman's home. A few days earlier, Hinman had sold the group the illegal drug mescaline, which they brought back to Spahn Ranch. Although Manson always had plenty of drugs around, this particular batch was meant for the use of the Straight Satans, an outlaw motorcycle gang that Manson was trying to recruit for security at the ranch.

The Straight Satans, however, were disappointed by what they had received from Hinman. They had provided the money for the drug buy, and now they wanted their money back. Manson wanted Hinman's money as well, believing what

Beausoleil had told him about Hinman's inheritance. Manson saw a good opportunity in Hinman to collect some easy cash.

When Beausoleil, Brunner, and another Family member, Susan "Sadie" Atkins, arrived at Hinman's home on July 25, Hinman welcomed them inside. The four sat around a kitchen table and talked. But their words grew unfriendly as Beausoleil started asking for money. When Hinman claimed he didn't have any, Beausoleil confronted him with a gun. During a struggle in the kitchen, the gun went off. Confusion and fighting followed. Hinman asked his troublesome visitors to leave, but they wouldn't.

Instead, Atkins used Hinman's phone to call Manson. Soon Manson and Bruce Davis, another Family member, arrived with a long, curved sword that Manson enjoyed playing with at Spahn Ranch. After repeating the demand for money and being refused, Manson slashed Hinman's ear with the sword, leaving a deep gash in the side of Hinman's head.

Then Manson left the house and returned to Spahn Ranch. But Beausoleil soon called him to explain that Hinman still wasn't cooperating. Manson instructed Beausoleil to "take care" of Hinman, who had been tied to a chair and was bleeding profusely from the cut to his head and ear.[2]

Despite Manson's instructions, Beausoleil hesitated. He had never hurt anyone deliberately. But leaving the house, or leaving Hinman, was going to be a problem. There was a good chance Hinman would go to the police, even if he claimed he wouldn't, and that could put both Beausoleil and Manson in jail. And Beausoleil knew what Manson wanted him to do. Beausoleil, Brunner, and Atkins stayed at the house for two days, until July 27, when Beausoleil used a buck knife to stab Hinman in his chest. After a few minutes, Hinman was dead.

THE FIRST VICTIM

On July 1, 1969, Family member Tex Watson met with drug dealer Bernard "Lotsapoppa" Crowe, supposedly to buy marijuana. But during the drug deal, Watson robbed Crowe. After the robbery, Crowe called Spahn Ranch and threatened the Family. In response, Manson went to Crowe's home and shot him. This made Crowe, who survived the attack, likely the first victim of Manson Family violence.

Beausoleil was mindful of Manson's preachings about the supposed impending race war, Helter Skelter. Before leaving Hinman's house, Beausoleil drew a cat's paw and the words *Political Piggy* on the wall in Hinman's blood. The idea was to convince the police that this murder was the act of the Black Panthers, an African American political group noted for its protests against racism and police brutality. Framing the Black Panthers for Hinman's death was seen as a way to potentially set off Manson's long-predicted race war.

Carelessly Arrested

Although Hinman didn't have any money, he did have a Fiat and a Volkswagen minibus. During the confrontation with the Manson Family, he had agreed to sign the vehicles over to Beausoleil. After the murder, Beausoleil used the Fiat as his own.

Hinman's body was discovered four days after he was killed. A few days later, on the morning of August 6, Beausoleil was sleeping in the back of the Fiat while on the side of Highway 101 near San Luis Obispo. A California Highway Patrol officer stopped to check on the car. When the officer asked Beausoleil a few questions, Beausoleil gave vague answers. The officer then ran the Fiat's license plates and found records that stated the car belonged to Gary Hinman, homicide victim. The officer arrested Beausoleil on suspicion of auto theft.

When police searched the car, they found a large buck knife hidden in the well holding the spare tire. Under questioning, Beausoleil admitted he had been at Hinman's house. He was then placed under arrest on suspicion of murder.

Manson knew Beausoleil's arrest meant a lot of trouble for the Family and for him personally. He knew that evidence from the Fiat, or Beausoleil's own words, could lead the police straight to Spahn Ranch. Under questioning, anyone who had been to Hinman's house could admit that Manson had

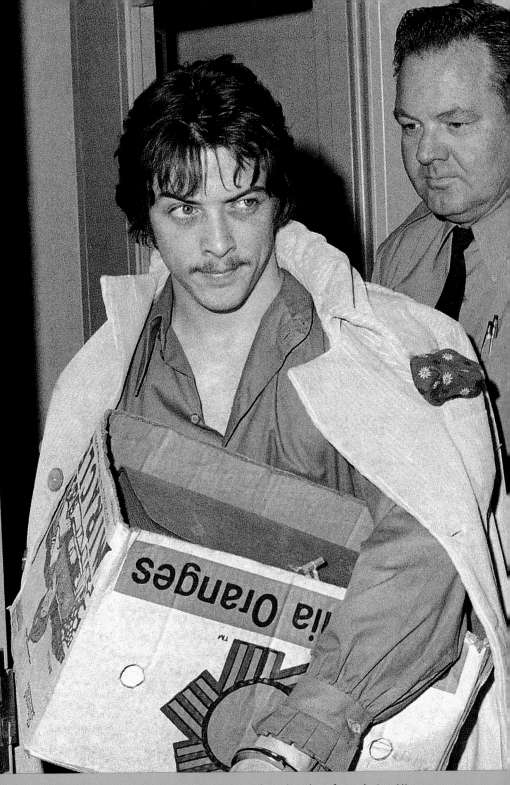

Beausoleil was found guilty of murdering Hinman.

assaulted Hinman. This would probably mean a long prison sentence for the Family's leader.

Manson felt himself losing control of the situation. Somehow, he had to keep a lid on this crime and keep the police away from Spahn Ranch. He had weapons at the ready and a group of people willing to kill for him. The time had come for Helter Skelter.

Inspirations for Helter Skelter

Throughout their time with Manson, the Family members eagerly listened for hours to his preachings. One of Manson's favorite subjects was the Book of Revelation, the last book of the Christian Bible's New Testament. Manson had very specific interpretations for some of its verses. He saw a deep connection between this ancient writing and the events of modern times. It helped shape his thoughts about Helter Skelter.

For Manson, a key verse from Revelation described a coming conflict that would bring the end of the world: "And the four angels were loosed, which were prepared for an hour, and a day, and a month, and a year, for to slay the third part of men."[3] This, in Manson's view, referred to what he called Helter Skelter. Manson believed that everyone would have to choose sides in this imminent conflict. He believed he and his followers could survive the race war by hiding in the desert.

Manson believed the four angels described in Revelation were the Beatles. He also believed their song lyrics had the power of prophecy, and he was especially obsessed with the album *The Beatles*, better known as *The White Album*. Manson had only general ideas about a coming race war before hearing *The White Album*. The concept of Helter Skelter came to Manson after this double-album Beatles recording came out in November 1968, including a song titled "Helter Skelter."

Manson interpreted "Helter Skelter" as a song about fighting, violence, and confusion. He believed several other songs on *The White Album* also described impending violence. In fact, Manson believed songs written by the Beatles were directly and purposefully linked to the Family and his own

THE HELTER SKELTER STORY

For its association with Charles Manson, "Helter Skelter" became one of the Beatles' most famous songs. It was a high-energy track written by Paul McCartney for *The White Album*. As McCartney explained to one interviewer, "That [song] came about just 'cause I'd read a review of a record which said, 'and this group really got us wild, there's echo on everything, they're screaming their heads off.' And I just remember thinking, 'Oh, it'd be great to do one ... really screaming record.'"[4] The song was never intended to be about a race war, though. *Helter-skelter* is actually a British term for an amusement park ride that consists of a giant spiral slide around a tower.

Manson imagined the world would fall into a violent conflict that he called "Helter Skelter." He preached about this belief to his Family members.

ideas. According to Manson, the song "Rocky Raccoon" referred to black people and the song "Sexy Sadie" referred to Susan "Sadie" Atkins. He said the song "Blackbird," although written as a soft and peaceful tune, was actually prompting the violent uprising of black people all over the world. Manson believed "Piggies" referred to the police, and the song inspired some of the Family's murder-scene writings. "Revolution 9," with its montage of strange sounds from a variety of sources and no lyrics, was a soundscape of the revolution to come, according to Manson.

Although Manson's beliefs about the impending Helter Skelter were entirely imaginary, the prediction of an imminent race conflict did not feel far-fetched to many of Manson's followers. Major riots had occurred in Los Angeles and other cities during the 1960s as people protested racism and police brutality. Paul Watkins, a member of the Family, later described Manson's race-war idea to prosecutor Vincent Bugliosi in court. "He used to explain how it would be so simple to start out," Watkins said. "A couple of black people . . . would come up into the Bel Air and Beverly Hills district . . . and just really wipe some people out, just cutting bodies up and smearing blood and writing things on the wall in blood."[5] Manson believed the outrage over these hypothetical killings would inspire fear and anger, and the fighting would gradually spread into Helter Skelter.

CHAPTER FIVE

HELTER SKELTER

I n the afternoon of August 8, 1969, Manson took Family member Tex Watson aside and gave him instructions. Later that evening, Watson and three other Family members climbed into a car and headed down Interstate 405, toward the Santa Monica Mountains and the hills and canyons just north of Beverly Hills. Their destination was 10050 Cielo Drive.

As the group headed south, Watson explained Manson's plan to the others—Patricia Krenwinkel, Susan Atkins, and Linda Kasabian. They arrived at the house around midnight. An electronic gate barred the driveway. Watson led the group around the gate on foot. He then spotted a car pulling away from the house and toward him. There was a single occupant—a young male driver—at the wheel.

Tex Watson, Manson Family member, in 1970

Watson walked up to the driver's side window and fired four shots from a .22-caliber Buntline Special revolver. The car's driver, Steve Parent, died almost instantly. Watson then led his group past the garage to the main house, where he cut a window screen so they could get inside. Watson then instructed Kasabian to stand guard at the gate.

Once inside the house, Atkins, Krenwinkel, and Watson rounded up the occupants: Sharon Tate, Abigail Folger, Jay Sebring, and Voytek Frykowski. They used a thick rope to tie up Tate and Sebring in the living room. When Sebring pleaded with the group, telling them that Tate was pregnant, Watson shot Sebring and stabbed him several times in his chest. Terrified, Folger and Frykowski ran out to the front lawn to escape. But their attackers chased them outside, stabbing and shooting, until Folger and Frykowski were left dying on the ground. Atkins and Watson then murdered Tate, ignoring her pleas for mercy. They stabbed her approximately 15 times with a buck knife.

The LaBianca Murders

The next night, Manson drove with Watson, Atkins, Kasabian, Krenwinkel, Steve Grogan, and Leslie Van Houten to the home of Rosemary and Leno LaBianca. Manson and Watson broke into the house and tied up the LaBiancas. Manson then left the house with Atkins, Kasabian, and Grogan. Meanwhile, Watson instructed Van Houten and Krenwinkel to help finish the killings. They grabbed knives from the kitchen and stabbed both LaBiancas to death.

Then they left the house and began hitchhiking back to Spahn Ranch. In the meantime, Manson, Atkins, Grogan, and Kasabian drove through Los Angeles, seeking out other victims. They did not kill anyone else, however. By the next morning, the entire group had returned to Spahn Ranch.

Gathering Evidence

Although the Tate and LaBianca murders received widespread attention, the police investigation of the killings progressed slowly. Detectives gathered a lot of evidence. At the Tate house, forensics technicians lifted many fingerprints. The prints didn't match those of any of the victims, the housekeeper, or William

ONE LESS VICTIM

In the early morning of August 9, 1969, Linda Kasabian stood guard while three of her companions murdered Sharon Tate and four others at 10050 Cielo Drive. On the next night, Kasabian watched while Manson directed the killing of the LaBiancas. Then Manson decided on one more victim for that night, Lebanese actor Saladin Nader. He handed a knife to Kasabian, who was an acquaintance of Nader. But when she reached Nader's apartment building, she deliberately went to the wrong door. This convinced Susan Atkins and Steve Grogan, who were with her, that the actor was not in the building. Nader was home that night, in fact, and Kasabian's actions probably saved his life.

Authorities pull a victim's body from the Tate house after the Manson Family murders there on August 9, 1969.

Garretson, the live-in caretaker. Investigators did not know whom the prints belonged to.

Police also took dozens of blood samples from the house, including from the living room, the sidewalks outside, and the front door. Some blood samples matched Jay Sebring, and others matched Sharon Tate. But still others did not match any of the victims.

The killers left some items at the Tate house that police collected as evidence. Investigators found a knife in one of Tate's living room chairs, and the killers had left a rope tied around two of the victims, Tate and Sebring. A pair of glasses was found at the scene as well. Investigators sent out bulletins to optical shops and asked several experts to examine the glasses. But the frames and the lenses were fairly common. They couldn't be traced to any specific doctor or store.

One clue in particular stuck out to officers—they found three pieces of a shattered gun grip at Tate's house, but no gun. The pieces were taken to the Firearms and Explosives unit of the LAPD's Scientific Investigation Department. Sergeant William Lee immediately identified the grip as a Hi-Standard. Lee contacted Ed Lomax, who worked for the company that owned Hi-Standard. Lomax identified the grip as belonging to the Buntline Special, a long-barreled revolver named after Ned Buntline, a nineteenth-century author of Western novels.

Only a few thousand of these guns had been made. Unable to locate the gun associated with the shattered grip, officers pursued other leads. But they couldn't seem to piece together what happened.

Missing the Links

At first, police did not see a link between the Tate, LaBianca, and Hinman murders. There were more than two dozen murders in Los Angeles on the weekend of the Tate and LaBianca murders. It was a hot summer—prime time for crime and homicide. Additionally, the three crime scenes were miles apart. The victims didn't know each other or have any business connections. At the Tate residence, investigators found marijuana, hashish, cocaine, and the synthetic drug MDA, indicating the possibility of a drug-related crime. But at the LaBianca residence, while many valuables were also left behind, there were not any drugs. There were words written in blood on the walls at both the Tate and LaBianca homes, but similar writing was also at the Hinman murder scene, for which Beausoleil was already in custody. Police suspected they may be dealing with copycat killers—people who were not connected to Beausoleil but were simply copying him.

As the investigation continued, speculation and rumors about the murders were rampant in the press. This was probably at least partly because one of the murder victims was a famous actress. One of the most common rumors was that the murders were committed by ritualistic or satanic cult members. Another theory involved a Hollywood drug party gone out of control. Some people also suspected Polanski, Tate's husband. The movie director had a noted interest in occult and horror movies. He was also known for his partying and boasting about having adulterous affairs. The fact that Polanski was in London at the time of the murders was seen by many as a too-convenient alibi.

The Missing Gun

On September 1, 1969, a few weeks after the Tate and LaBianca murders, a ten-year-old boy named Steven Weiss was working in the backyard of his parents' home in the Sherman Oaks neighborhood of Los Angeles. Steven found something surprising in the yard—it looked like an old Western gun with a long, thin barrel. The gun

POLANSKI AND THE BLOODSTAINED WALLS

Although Roman Polanski was deeply depressed by his wife's murder, he still accepted an offer from *Life* magazine to publicly talk about what happened. A *Life* writer and photographer interviewed Polanski at the Cielo Drive house. One of the photos showed Polanski kneeling by the front door of his house with bloodstains still on the walk and the word *Pig* written in Sharon Tate's blood still visible on the door.

lay halfway up a steep hill, near Beverly Glen Boulevard. This winding road stretches across the Santa Monica Mountains and into the Beverly Hills neighborhood.

When he saw the gun, Steven's father contacted police. Officers soon confiscated the firearm. The gun was a nine-shot Hi-Standard revolver with seven spent casings and two live rounds. The barrel was slightly bent, and the gun was missing part of its grip.

A few days later, by coincidence, the LAPD sent out alerts about the gun they were searching for based on the three pieces of its broken grip that were found at the Tate crime scene. But the alert did not reach the LAPD facility in the

COLONEL TATE'S INVESTIGATION

Sharon Tate's death devastated her father, Paul "PJ" Tate. Lieutenant Colonel Paul Tate was a military veteran who had served 23 years in US Army intelligence. He decided to apply that knowledge to investigating his daughter's murder.

Following the theory that the murder was linked to illegal narcotics, Tate dressed himself like a drug-seeking hippie and went undercover. He spent several months hanging out at clubs and parties in Los Angeles and San Francisco, seeking clues to whom the killers might be. "Action quiets the mind," Tate said in his family's book *Restless Souls*. "I could no more sit around waiting for the LAPD to solve Sharon's case than I could leave a downed soldier to die alone in the field."[1]

Although he was on the right track by moving in the counterculture underground, Tate was unable to come up with any solid leads. He did manage to uncover a major drug operation, but the police investigators told him to stay out of their case.

Van Nuys neighborhood, where the gun found by Steven Weiss was held. For the time being, the gun was stowed away while the Van Nuys officers decided what to do with it.

In the meantime, friends of Tate took matters into their own hands by offering up the $25,000 reward. They announced it through a notice printed in the *Los Angeles Times*. In general, the Los Angeles police, and other police departments, don't really favor the offering of such private rewards, no matter how famous the sponsors. The result, in the case of the Tate homicide, was as usual: a wave of false leads and confessions that didn't give investigators any better information or evidence than they already had.

CHAPTER SIX

CLOSING IN ON THE FAMILY

The LaBianca, Tate, and Hinman murders were not the only deaths that occurred at the hands of the Manson Family. There was one more killing. The August 16 raid on Spahn Ranch had resulted in the arrest of more than two dozen suspected auto thieves. But because the officers had waited three days to stage the raid, the warrant they used—signed by a judge on August 13—had expired. This made the warrant invalid and any evidence collected inadmissible in court. All charges were dropped, and Manson and his Family were released. At the time of the raid, none of them was yet suspected of murder.

Inside one of the Spahn Ranch buildings where members of the Manson Family lived

The Murder of Shorty Shea

Upon release, Manson had some business to take care of back at Spahn Ranch. On Manson's orders, Watson and two other Family members attacked one of George Spahn's employees, Donald "Shorty" Shea. After hitting Shea, they drove down Santa Susana Pass with him and eventually pulled over to the side of the road. There, Manson and the others stabbed Shea to death.

Manson did not like Shea for several reasons. First, Manson and several of his followers suspected that Shea had been talking to the police and may have cooperated with them in planning the August 16 raid. Second, Shea seemed openly hostile to the Family and wanted to kick them off the ranch. Also, Shea was married to a black woman, which Manson considered a very serious offense.

Shea's sudden disappearance raised some questions at Spahn Ranch. Although Shea was known to disappear for

FINDING SHORTY SHEA

The location of Shorty Shea's body remained a mystery until 1977, when Family member Steve Grogan, convicted of participating in Shea's murder, accepted a deal from the Los Angeles County Sheriff's Office. If Grogan could lead investigators to Shea's grave, he would get a decent chance at being released from prison on parole. Grogan brought the police to skeletal remains on the former Spahn Ranch. The body was determined to be Shea's. In 1985, after serving 15 years behind bars, Grogan was released on parole.[1]

weeks at a time, there were rumors going around that he had been murdered. Although Manson's leadership of the Family was never in question, he could not prevent his followers from talking.

In the Desert

With the arrest of Beausoleil, the raid on Spahn Ranch, and the gossip around the ranch about Shea's death and the other murders, things were getting dangerous for Manson, who was growing more paranoid and more violent. Believing the killings were set to bring about Helter Skelter, Manson decided to carry out a long-planned move to the hot deserts of Death Valley, approximately 250 miles (402 km) northeast of Spahn Ranch.

The Family made its new home in the desert at a couple of mining outposts, Barker Ranch and Myers Ranch. These camps were so isolated that they were essentially free of law enforcement. That made it easier to talk openly about the crimes that had happened back in Los Angeles. Atkins, the murderer of Sharon Tate, and Van Houten, who took part in the LaBianca killings, often bragged about how much fun murder had been. Several other Family members began to realize that joining Manson was not what they had hoped for and started planning to escape.

Some succeeded in their escapes, hoping to put as much distance as possible between themselves and California law

Barker Ranch, shown in 2008, has been abandoned in the years since the Manson Family lived there.

enforcement. Tex Watson returned to his home state of Texas. Linda Kasabian had already left the group at Spahn Ranch, heading to New Mexico and then to New England.

Family members Kitty Lutesinger and Stephanie Schram tried to hitchhike out from the Death Valley outposts, but they were picked up by deputies from the Inyo County Sheriff's Department. Taken into custody and questioned, Lutesinger revealed that Atkins had taken part in the killing of Hinman. Inyo County authorities notified investigators in Los Angeles.

Busted for Arson

Meanwhile, at Barker Ranch, Manson kept his followers as isolated from civilization and law enforcement as possible. The group dug hideouts in the rocky hills, set up camouflaged lookouts, and used walkie-talkies to communicate.

Manson continued his regular evening lectures. A prominent theme was his theory about a bottomless pit. Somewhere in the vast desert, Manson believed, was a place of safety, a vast underground cavern where the entire Family could wait out Helter Skelter. When it was all over, Manson preached, they would emerge to a better time and a better place.

Spahn Ranch was destroyed by a wildfire in 1970. The property where it sat is now part of the Santa Susanna Pass State Historic Park.

During the day, the Family rode the nearby trails in dune buggies to set up lookouts and hideouts as a safety precaution. Manson and his followers considered the camps, and everything found there, to be their property. On one occasion, when they found an unattended construction loader, which they considered to be a disruption, they set it on fire.

Park rangers soon found the charred remains of the vehicle. In investigating the fire, park ranger Richard Powell stopped

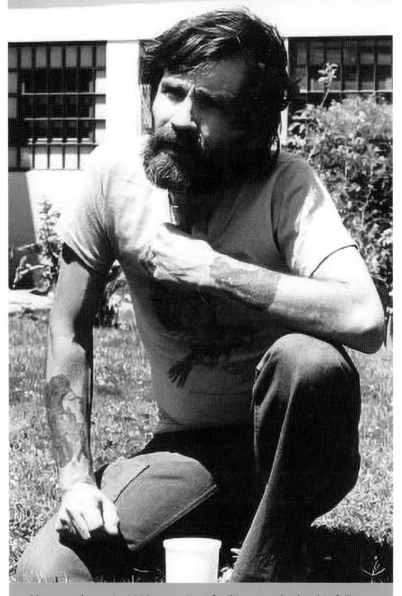

Manson, shown in 1980 at a prison facility, preached to his followers nearly every night in the late 1960s.

a red Toyota four-wheel drive vehicle in the area. He talked with the people inside, five Family members. Powell believed they might be linked to the construction loader arson, so he ran the vehicle's plates. Suspiciously, it was registered to Gail

Beausoleil, the wife of Bobby Beausoleil, who was in jail at the time for murdering Hinman.

Through talking with other people who lived in the area, the rangers had learned about Manson's camps at Barker Ranch and Myers Ranch. Local miners, angry at the disruption brought by the Family, were eager to help with the arson investigation. On October 12, authorities raided both camps. They arrested Manson, Atkins, and several other Family members. When the officers found Manson, he was hiding in the cupboard of a ramshackle cabin.

MUSIC BEHIND BARS

It turns out that Bobby Beausoleil made it a bit further in the music industry than Charles Manson. Although sentenced to life in prison for the murder of Gary Hinman, he didn't stop making music. He formed a series of bands while in prison and has released several studio albums, including *Voodoo Shivaya*, recorded at the Oregon State Penitentiary over seven years and released in 2018.[2] His most well-known album, *Lucifer Rising*, released in 1980, was also recorded in prison.

CHAPTER SEVEN

MAKING
THE CASE

hough Manson and several of his Family members were arrested, they still had not officially been linked to the Tate and LaBianca murders. But the police were beginning to piece everything together. In the Los Angeles women's jail that housed Atkins, inmates had plenty of time for conversation. On November 6, Atkins got fellow inmate Virginia Graham interested in her story about the murder of Sharon Tate and four other people in a swanky neighborhood of western Los Angeles. Like everyone else in the country, Graham knew about that crime. In fact, she felt closer to it than most other people. She had once met Sebring, one of the victims, and while looking for a house to rent, she had visited 10050 Cielo Drive.

Graham was fascinated, then terrified, by Atkins's description of the killing. There was no hesitation on Atkins's part—only pride. She told Graham about how Watson had

A law enforcement officer escorts Susan Atkins, a Manson Family member, into a courtroom.

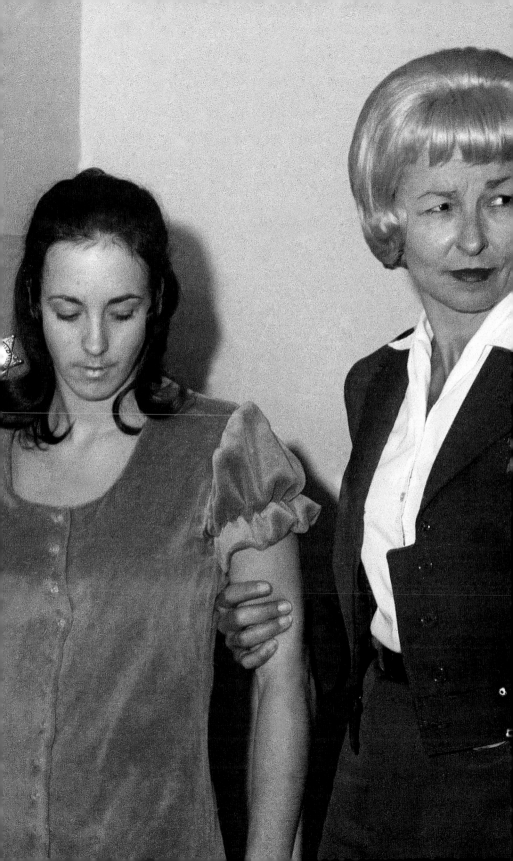

given orders to the group, how they had surprised the victims in the house late at night, and how she had stabbed Tate to death despite the actress's pleas for mercy. Graham later told the story to inmate Ronnie Howard, who notified the prison's authorities.

Meanwhile, Los Angeles city and county homicide detectives were pulling several other threads together. Bernard Weiss, the father of Steven Weiss, had called the police after reading about the gun missing from the Tate murder scene.

The .22-caliber Hi-Standard gun used in the Tate murders became part of a collection of evidence used against the Manson Family members in court.

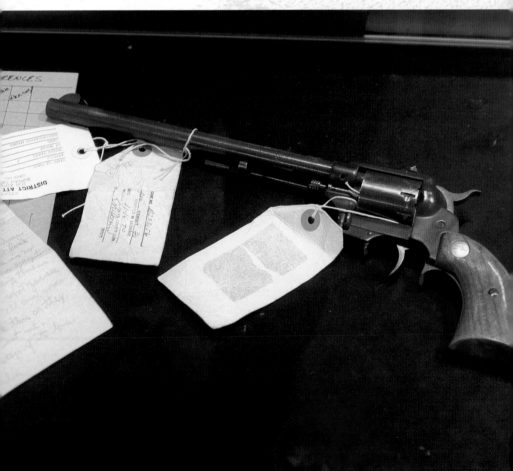

He described the weapon his son had found in his backyard in Sherman Oaks. The .22-caliber Hi-Standard was still locked away at the police department's Van Nuys station. The homicide detectives retrieved the gun and identified it as the weapon used to kill Parent and Sebring.

The police also had information from residents and workers at Spahn Ranch who had overheard Manson and others talking about murder. A week after Atkins's revealing conversation with Virginia Graham, Straight Satans biker Danny DeCarlo told authorities that Manson had murdered Shorty Shea. DeCarlo had also heard talk about the murders of Tate and the others at Cielo Drive, but he was reluctant to testify to it in court.

In order to win a conviction on murder, prosecutors need to establish guilt "beyond a reasonable doubt."[1] They need more than hearsay testimony—things overheard and accounts of casual conversations. In the case of the Tate and LaBianca murders, establishing guilt was going to be difficult.

Talking to the Grand Jury

By the end of November 1969, the Los Angeles County District Attorney's Office believed it had enough evidence to bring a case against Manson and the Family for several murders. On November 18, the district attorney assigned prosecutor Vincent Bugliosi to the Tate and LaBianca murders. It was Bugliosi's job to pull together evidence and witness testimonies

Prosecutor Vincent Bugliosi, *left*, and another representative of the district attorney's office speak to the press about the gun used in the Tate murders.

in order to convince a jury that the Family members were guilty. Bugliosi led searches of Spahn Ranch and Barker Ranch, where the police collected .22-caliber bullet casings. They had also collected many guns in previous raids, and they had fingerprints and other physical evidence that connected several members of the Manson Family to the crime scenes.

But aside from this physical evidence, Bugliosi also needed testimony, under oath and on the witness stand in court, regarding exactly what happened. He offered a deal to Atkins— prosecutors would not seek the death penalty in her case in return for her sworn testimony. Atkins agreed to testify before a grand jury, a group that meets in a closed session and decides whether to bring criminal charges against an accused defendant.

On December 1, authorities publicly announced that the case of the Tate and LaBianca murders had been solved, with criminal charges expected for Charles Manson, Tex Watson, Susan Atkins, Patricia Krenwinkel, Linda Kasabian, and Leslie Van Houten. All but Watson and

BUGLIOSI ON THE CASE

Prosecutor Bugliosi had a strong record of convictions. Out of more than 100 cases he prosecuted, he failed to win a conviction in only one of them. After the Manson case, Bugliosi also became a best-selling author. His book about the Manson case, *Helter Skelter: The True Story of the Manson Murders*, has sold more than seven million copies.[2]

Kasabian were already in custody. Within a few days, Kasabian surrendered in New Hampshire. Watson, apprehended in Texas, pursued a legal process to contest being transferred to California to appear in court.

The grand jury hearing happened on December 5. Atkins's testimony offered full details of the murder at 10050 Cielo Drive. She also spoke in detail about her own history with Manson. The Family's leader was incredibly persuasive, offering suggestions that Atkins and the others eagerly followed. No matter what Manson asked, Atkins testified, she and the others would carry it out. "Starting about a year ago," Atkins said at the beginning of her testimony, "he said, 'I have tricked all of you. I have tricked you into doing what I want you to and I am using you and you are all aware of that now and it is like I have got a bunch of slaves around me,' and he often called us sheep."[3] The information from this testimony convinced the grand jury to criminally charge Manson, Watson, Atkins, Krenwinkel, Van Houten, and Kasabian.

Kasabian's Testimony

While Watson was still in Texas, Manson and the others prepared to go on trial for murder in California. With their Death Valley outposts being watched by law enforcement, the rest of the Family began to scatter. But many remained loyal

Linda Kasabian speaks at a press conference after testifying in court.

to Manson. He stayed in contact with these followers through phone calls and messages sent through visitors.

In the meantime, Bugliosi spent the next few months working on the case, pulling together all of the evidence. With fingerprints taken from Family members now in custody, investigators positively identified two fingerprints at the Tate residence: Krenwinkel and Watson. The murder gun had been found as well, and in December, a television news crew had found bloodstained clothing in the hills near the Tate residence.

Searching for more direct testimony he could use in court, Bugliosi turned to Kasabian. Although Kasabian had been at the Cielo Drive murder scene, investigators determined that she hadn't killed anyone herself. This made her a better witness, in Bugliosi's view, than Atkins. The district attorney's office agreed to offer Kasabian complete immunity from prosecution, meaning she would no longer be charged with murder. But in return, Kasabian would have to tell Bugliosi everything she knew. She also would have to get on the witness stand and repeat her testimony in front of a jury—and Manson.

Kasabian had served as a lookout at 10050 Cielo Drive on the night of the murders. Upset by the violence, she had tried, but failed, to distract Watson, Atkins, and Krenwinkel by claiming people were on their way to the house. Kasabian had a detailed

THE HELTER SKELTER TOUR

Hollywood tourists flock to guided tours about the city's famed entertainment industry and history. The murders carried out by Manson and the Family are no exception. The Helter Skelter tour occurs every Saturday morning. The tour visits sites connected to the Tate and LaBianca murders—including El Coyote, the Mexican restaurant on Beverly Boulevard where Sharon Tate had her last meal—with accompanying audio and video clips.

understanding of what had happened. Bugliosi interviewed her several times in jail and took her out of her holding cell on a ride through the canyons north of Los Angeles. The intent was to jog Kasabian's memory and get her to corroborate the evidence and the timeline that investigators had developed in the case.

At Cielo Drive, Kasabian pointed out where Watson had cut telephone wires. She showed where she and the others had climbed a hill through trees and brush to get around the front gate. She had not entered the house, but she did see Frykowski and Folger chased out of the house and stabbed to death on the lawn. She also showed where Parent was shot in his car. She described the guns and knives that the group had with them that night. She also pointed out where they had ditched their clothes and disposed of the gun.

Finally, Kasabian described what happened at Spahn Ranch after the group arrived. Manson had asked the four whether they had any remorse for their actions. None said that they did. "I was afraid for my life," she told Bugliosi. "I could see in [Manson's] eyes he knew how I felt."[4] Kasabian's story lined up with every piece of physical evidence held by the investigators.

CHAPTER EIGHT

THE TRIAL

The murder trial of Manson, Krenwinkel, Atkins, and Van Houten began on June 15, 1970, in Los Angeles. Each of the four defendants had the right to an attorney. In cases where a defendant can't or does not want to pay for an attorney, the court appoints a public defender. At first, Manson would not accept his court-appointed lawyer. The judge allowed Manson to represent himself in court during pretrial procedures.

However, angry and disruptive, Manson staged several outbursts, ridiculing the court and the judge, interrupting the prosecutors, and making demands. This behavior convinced the judge that an attorney would be necessary to rein in Manson. Manson agreed to have Irving Kanarek as his court-appointed attorney, but Manson carved an *X* into his own forehead as a sign of protest. The other defendants and several followers who attended the trial followed their leader by carving the letter *X* into their foreheads as well.

Three law enforcement officers escort Manson into court.

A CHANGE IN ATTITUDE

In the view of many, the Manson Family murders marked a violent end to the 1960s and to the promise of the counterculture that the world was at the dawn of a new era of peace and love. Hippie culture started going out of fashion as the world became a more violent, strange, and chaotic place. In Los Angeles, a center for the movie industry, the crime also caused a change in attitude. Julian Wasser, a Hollywood photographer who accompanied Roman Polanski to the Cielo Drive house just after the murders, explained how his own profession changed:

> It wasn't like it is now: there were no paparazzi, no VIP sections, no security. It was a really innocent time. You'd just walk up and there they were. They'd stop and smile and pose. Now it's a business. If you want exclusive access to a celebrity, you have to pay big money. You weren't considered some sort of psychotic menace who's going to rob or kill them either. Now they'll call their security person and you'll get beat up. Now you go to a party in LA and you have the right badge or you're just some slob. . . . It's a rough world now. I think Manson started it and . . . reality has fallen on us like a ton of bricks.[2]

It took 24 trial days to select the 12 jurors who would decide the case.[1] An important requirement for any juror is that he or she cannot have formed an opinion on the guilt or innocence of the accused. With the Tate and LaBianca murders all over the news for the previous ten months, finding people who could view the trial with an open mind was difficult.

Contempt of Court

After the trial began, as the lawyers made their arguments and questioned witnesses, Manson continued to be disruptive. On one occasion, he rushed toward the judge and threatened his life, shouting, "In the name of Christian justice, someone should cut your head off!"[3] Another time, Manson held up a newspaper with a headline clear to the judge, jury, and everyone in the courtroom: "Manson Guilty, Nixon Declares."[4] According to the newspaper article, President Richard Nixon himself had spoken out on the case, pointing to Manson as guilty, despite the fact that no one had yet been declared guilty in court.

Defense attorneys immediately stood to move for a mistrial. Manson's actions were clearly unacceptable. But now that the jury had seen an opinion on the case from the president of the United States, the defense attorneys claimed there was no chance the jurors could serve as impartial deciders on the case.

The judge ordered the jurors out of the room. Each of them was asked whether they could continue to serve impartially. Each answered yes. The trial resumed, but not before the judge found Dave Shinn, one of the defense attorneys, guilty of contempt for allowing Manson to grab the newspaper. He sentenced Shinn to jail for three days.

Dangerous Testimony

For witnesses, testifying in court against Manson carried real danger. Family member Barbara Hoyt had information about Manson's words and actions on the night of the Tate killing. She had also heard screaming during Shea's murder and had heard Atkins confess to killing Tate. Hoyt was not a defendant in the case, but prosecutors still wanted her to testify as a witness.

However, by early September, Hoyt was still uncertain about whether she should testify in court under oath.

Hoyt had a tempting offer from other Family members. If she kept quiet, they would pay for her to travel to Hawaii. Hoyt accepted and left for Hawaii with several other Family members. They spent a few days in the islands, then prepared to return to California. Before going to the airport, Hoyt's companions spiked a hamburger with the drug LSD and gave it to her. Suffering intense hallucinations, Hoyt collapsed in the street and nearly died from the overdose. She was found and brought to a hospital. After recovering, she approached Bugliosi and declared herself ready to testify.

Paul Watkins was also willing to talk in court. Although he had left Spahn Ranch by the time of the murders, he still hung out with the Family and had valuable information about Manson. From Watkins, Bugliosi learned about Helter Skelter, Manson's fascination with the Beatles, and Manson's belief in an impending race war. Watkins was more than willing to take the stand and testify, despite threats from Family members. "Charlie was always preaching love," Watkins said. "Charlie had no idea what love was. Charlie was so far from love it wasn't even funny. Death is Charlie's trip. It really is."[5] Watkins's testimony was important in establishing Manson's motive and in showing how Manson controlled and directed his followers. But Watkins's departure from the Manson Family may have

Former Manson Family member Barbara Hoyt arrives at court to testify.

nearly cost him his life. One night while Watkins was sleeping in his van, a suspicious fire broke out in the vehicle, nearly killing him.

Not Going Quietly

Throughout the trial, Manson's outbursts and protests continued. Nevertheless, Bugliosi and the prosecution team pressed on with testimony from police, investigators, and other witnesses from both inside and outside the Family. On January 13, 1971, after calling 84 witnesses to the stand over nearly seven months, Bugliosi gave his closing statement.[6] The prosecution then rested its case. The details of the murders were clear, and the prosecutor believed the guilt of Manson and the other defendants had been clearly established.

Once the prosecution rests, the defense team has its chance to call witnesses, present evidence, and make a case that guilt has not been proven. But the lawyers representing the Family declared they would not present any case at all. This caused another outbreak in the courtroom. The defendants shouted their own objections. They wanted to testify to share their side of the story, no matter what their own lawyers said. Judge Charles Older called a recess and met with the attorneys in his chambers.

Attorneys for the three women on trial did not want them to testify because doing so meant they would have to face

From left, Susan Atkins, Patricia Krenwinkel and Leslie Van Houten

cross-examination from prosecutors. With all the evidence of their actions already placed in the record, defense attorneys believed the inevitable result would be self-incrimination— an admission of guilt. Witnesses and defendants have a constitutional right to remain silent if what they say could be self-incriminating. However, if their sworn testimony is offered voluntarily during a trial, they have no right to refuse to answer

Ronald Hughes, the defense attorney for Leslie Van Houten, was not willing to let his client testify. Like the other defense attorneys, he believed such testimony would amount to a confession. "I refuse to take part in any proceeding where I am forced to push a client out the window," he said.[7] This didn't help Manson, who wanted Van Houten and others to testify he had nothing to do with the murders.

The court adjourned that week for a long Thanksgiving weekend. On the following Monday, attorneys, defendants, and court officials returned, ready to bring the trial to an end. Hughes, however, was missing. He had gone camping that weekend and went missing after a violent storm flooded the park where he was staying. Hughes was later found dead. People widely suspected the Manson Family had something to do with his death, but authorities ruled out that possibility.

further questions based on that testimony. They must answer, no matter how incriminating their words might be.

The defense attorneys believed Atkins, Krenwinkel, and Van Houten were still heavily under Manson's influence. They believed the women would testify that they had planned and carried out the murders on their own. This would put Manson in the clear and the other defendants on their way to a guilty verdict and a death sentence.

Judge Older ruled that the defendants could testify. Manson then spoke up, saying he wanted to make a statement. Older ordered the jurors out of the room.

From the witness stand, Manson spoke for more than an hour, claiming he had no responsibility for any of the deaths carried out by his followers. He said:

Most of the people at the ranch that you call the Family were just people that you did not want, people that were alongside the road, that their parents had kicked out, that did not want to go to Juvenile Hall. So I did the best I could and I took them up on my garbage dump and I told them this: that in love there is no wrong. . . . I told them that anything they do for their brothers and sisters is good if they do it with a good thought. . . . It's not my conspiracy, it's not my music. . . . It says 'Rise,' it says 'Kill.' Why blame it on me? I didn't write the music.[8]

After Manson finished speaking, he stood up and left the witness stand. Turning to the women at the defense table, he said, "You don't have to testify now."[9]

CHAPTER NINE

THE VERDICTS

O n January 15, 1971, after a trial that had lasted seven months, the fate of Charles Manson and three of his followers was turned over to a jury. Although the defense attorneys did not call any witnesses, they had not simply given up. They made their own closing arguments, speaking at length on the strange circumstances of the crime. They harped on the vague and conflicting testimony surrounding Manson's instructions to his Family members. They described Manson's strange philosophy as perhaps eccentric but not criminal.

Kanarek, Manson's attorney, delivered a summation that lasted seven days. Kanarek accused Kasabian of lying to escape prosecution. The Family members were on trial for the Tate and LaBianca murders, and in those cases, Kanarek pointed out, Manson had personally harmed no one. Manson's attorney argued: if Manson had simply delivered an opinion on a supposed coming race war, and the way it might start, did

Manson is escorted back to jail by law enforcement officers after a court hearing.

that make him guilty of murder if misguided people took him too literally?

The Death Penalty

The jury returned ten days later with its verdict: guilty on all counts. Manson himself was found guilty based on the legal grounds of conspiracy—aiding and abetting a plan to commit murder. Then the final phase of the trial had arrived: sentencing. In California at that time, first-degree murder convictions could be punished by a death sentence.

While incarcerated, Manson continued to attract fans and followers. He set a record for most mail received by any inmate in the California prison system.

Once convicted, one of the defendants, Van Houten, moved for an insanity defense, which means she asked to be found not guilty by reason of insanity. Her attorney, Maxwell Keith, asked the court to appoint a psychiatrist to evaluate her. Keith claimed that Van Houten had no will of her own. Coming under Manson's sway, Keith argued, Van Houten's inability to make decisions meant she wasn't responsible for her own acts. The judge refused this plea, but Keith wasn't finished. He argued for a ruling that the death penalty itself was unconstitutional, a violation of the Eighth Amendment ban on "cruel and unusual punishment."[1] This motion was also denied.

On March 29, the jury decided to sentence all of the defendants to the death penalty. Krenwinkel, Atkins, and Van Houten were moved to the California Institution for Women, in the town of Corona. Manson was incarcerated on death row at the San Quentin State Prison on San Francisco Bay. The prison was just a few miles from the Haight-Ashbury neighborhood of San Francisco, where the Family had begun.

Meanwhile, Watson's appeals against being transferred to California had failed. In February 1971, he stood trial on his own for the Tate and LaBianca murders. While in jail during his trial, Watson was a troublesome inmate. He refused to eat most foods, lost weight, hardly spoke, and became unable or unwilling to respond to any questions. Although his attorney mounted an insanity defense, Watson was deemed to have been legally sane at the time of the murders as well as during the trial. The jury in his case pronounced him guilty in October and also sentenced him to the death penalty.

Manson and the other Family members appealed their convictions and sentences through the court system, but all of these efforts failed. Then, in 1972, a case heard in the California Supreme Court resulted in a ruling that made the death penalty illegal in the state. The

Leslie Van Houten holds the Family record for parole denials. As of early 2019, she had been denied parole 21 times.[2]

sentences of all inmates on death row, including the members of the Manson Family, were changed to life in prison. After serving a minimum prison time, they would all have a chance at parole. In the years after their trial, these Family members would repeatedly apply to be released on parole. But as of early 2019, parole had never been granted. Atkins died in prison in 2009. In 2017, Manson also died in prison. He was 83.

The Motive

In the years since Manson's conviction, even as he sat in prison, a clear motive for his crimes has never emerged. He may have targeted homes of wealthy people to set off Helter Skelter, but there were thousands of such homes in Los Angeles. Why did he choose 10050 Cielo Drive and the LaBianca residence?

VICTIMS' RIGHTS

In the years that have passed since the Manson Family murders, relatives of the victims have regularly showed up at parole hearings, arguing against the release of convicted Family members. At one such hearing in 1976, Sharon Tate's sister, Debra Tate, became the first person in California to deliver a victim impact statement. This type of official statement explains to a court the effect of a crime on the victims and their families. California passed the Victims' Bill of Rights in 1982, which allowed victim impact statements to be read in court. This law was effectively supported by Doris Tate, Sharon Tate's mother, who became a prominent advocate for crime victims' rights. The passing of California's law bolstered efforts to improve victims' rights across the country. Victim impact statements are now permitted by law in all 50 states.

A likely explanation for targeting the LaBianca house is that members of the Family had hung out there before the LaBiancas moved into the house. As for the Tate residence, Bugliosi, who knew the case well, offers a guess in his book *Helter Skelter*. Manson had been to 10050 Cielo Drive a couple of times before the murder. On March 23, 1969, he went to the house looking for music producer Terry Melcher. Altobelli, the owner of the house, was staying in the guesthouse that day. He explained to Manson that Melcher no longer lived there. He lied and said he didn't have Melcher's new address in Malibu. Altobelli didn't like or trust Manson, and he didn't want him coming back to the Cielo Drive house. As Manson was usually surrounded by obedient followers, he wasn't used to people turning him away or confronting him. Although Bugliosi had no way to prove it, he believed this encounter

THE LAST TRIAL

After his conviction, Manson served time in several different California institutions. He spent his last years at the state prison in Corcoran. Although he asked 12 times for parole, he was denied every time. On November 19, 2017, he died from cancer and cardiac arrest.

After Manson died, there was still one more courtroom trial. Four different men claimed the rights to Manson's body, saying either they were related to Manson or had a valid will leaving them the body. After a jury trial, the court decided for Jason Freeman, who claimed to be Manson's grandson, to keep the body. Freeman said his intention was to have the body cremated.

may have prompted negative feelings against 10050 Cielo Drive for Manson. "Not only were these people obviously establishment, they were establishment in the very fields— entertainment, recording, motion pictures—in which Manson had tried to make it and failed," Bugliosi wrote.[3]

Manson's Legacy

While Manson spent the rest of his life behind bars, he achieved notoriety as one of the most famous killers in history. His story has inspired many newspaper and magazine stories, books, and movies. He also continues to have a cultlike following of Manson obsessives, fans who have spent long hours and many

After being convicted of murder, Manson spent the rest of his life in prison. He routinely carved a swastika, the symbol of Adolf Hitler's Nazi Party during World War II, into his forehead.

MANSON COLLECTIBLES

Ever since his arrest and conviction, Charles Manson has provided a hot market for collectors. Letters and postcards signed by Manson can be purchased online. However, the sale of this "murderabilia," or personal effects of famous criminals, doesn't fascinate everyone. Andy Kahan, a crime victims' advocate from Houston, Texas, has spoken out against the sale and collection of these types of items, stating that it is insensitive to crime victims and darkly promotional of gruesome crimes. "It's one of the most egregious things I've seen after being involved in the criminal justice system for 25 years," Kahan said in 2011. "I was just stunned and mortified [to learn] that individuals can commit these types of offenses and go on to further claim infamy and immortality."[4]

years poring over every detail of the case. Dozens of websites are devoted to Manson, and collectors trade memorabilia and mementos of his crimes.

Manson became a symbol of his time and place in history. The Manson Family murders occurred at the end of the turbulent 1960s. During this era, many young people participated in the counterculture by living communally, following gurus in new philosophies and religions, making new kinds of music, and striving for a future of peace and enlightenment. But in many ways, this hopeful future never came. Instead, a guru from San Francisco, a city at the center of the counterculture, came to symbolize something very different: mindless violence, evil, and murder.

TIMELINE

1934

- Charles Manson is born in Cincinnati, Ohio.

1940s

- Manson is held in various juvenile reformatories and commits petty crimes.

1951

- Manson escapes from a reformatory and travels to the West Coast with two companions, robbing gas stations along the way for money.

1960

- Manson begins serving a ten-year prison sentence after being convicted of forgery.

1967

- Manson is released on parole and moves to San Francisco.

1968

- A group of Manson's followers known as the Family move to Los Angeles. They eventually move to the Spahn Movie Ranch in the Simi Hills area of northern Los Angeles County.

1969

- On July 1, Family member Tex Watson tries to rob Los Angeles drug dealer Bernard "Lotsapoppa" Crowe. This leads to Manson shooting Crowe, who survives.

- On July 27, Gary Hinman is murdered by Manson Family member Bobby Beausoleil. A few days later, Beausoleil is arrested and charged with the murder.

- On August 8, Family members arrive at 10050 Cielo Drive and kill Sharon Tate, Abigail Folger, Voytek Frykowski, Jay Sebring, and Steve Parent.

- On August 10, several members of the Family kill Rosemary and Leno LaBianca in their home in the Los Feliz neighborhood of Los Angeles.

- On August 16, the Los Angeles County Sheriff's Department raids the Spahn ranch, taking Manson and his followers into custody on suspicion of auto theft. All are later released due to a misdated search warrant.

- In October, the Family's new residence of Barker Ranch in Death Valley is raided. Manson and his followers are arrested again on suspicion of auto theft and arson.

- In December, after the police gather evidence and witness testimonies in the Tate/LaBianca murder case, Manson and four of his followers are formally charged with first-degree murder.

1970

- On June 15, the murder trial of Charles Manson, Patricia Krenwinkel, Susan Atkins, and Leslie Van Houten begins.

1971

- On January 25, Manson and the other defendants are found guilty on all counts.

- In March, Manson, Krenwinkel, Atkins, and Van Houten are sentenced to the death penalty.

- In October, Tex Watson is sentenced to the death penalty after being tried and convicted separately in relation to the Tate/LaBianca murders.

1972

- California repeals the death penalty, and the sentences of Manson and the Family members are reduced to life imprisonment.

2017

- Manson dies in prison.

ESSENTIAL FACTS

SIGNIFICANT EVENTS

- The followers of Charles Manson committed a series of violent murders in the summer of 1969. These crimes included the killing of actress Sharon Tate, which occurred on the night of August 8.

- Manson and members of his Family were arrested at their Death Valley encampment known as the Barker Ranch on October 12, 1969. Although they were initially booked into jail on suspicion of auto theft and arson, they would eventually be charged with murder.

- The trial of Charles Manson and three of his followers for first-degree murder began in June 1970. The trial lasted nine months, resulting in all defendants being found guilty.

- Charles Manson died in 2017. He continued to proclaim his innocence in the 1969 murders, based on the fact that he didn't personally participate in them.

KEY PLAYERS

- Charles Manson led a cult of followers, known as the Manson Family, to commit crimes, including killing eight people.

- Sharon Tate, a famous actress, was one of five people murdered by the Manson Family in her Los Angeles home.

- Leno and Rosemary LaBianca were both killed in their home by the Manson Family shortly after the murders at Tate's home.

- Susan Atkins, one of the many young women who followed Manson, participated in the Tate/LaBianca murders.

- Vincent Bugliosi, a Los Angeles County attorney, prosecuted the case against the Manson Family.

IMPACT ON SOCIETY

The horrific Manson Family murders shocked the nation. They frightened many in the Hollywood entertainment industry and tarnished the 1960s counterculture revolution with bloody violence. Charles Manson became one of the country's most notorious criminals.

QUOTE

"Charlie had no idea what love was. Charlie was so far from love it wasn't even funny. Death is Charlie's trip. It really is."

—*Paul Watkins, member of the Manson Family, in 1970*

GLOSSARY

alibi
A claim that proves an accused person could not be guilty of a crime.

arson
The illegal act of intentionally setting fire to a building or other structure.

commune
A place where people live together in a group, sharing possessions.

counterculture
A culture of values that go against those of established society, popularized in the 1960s.

death row
The area of a prison reserved for those sentenced to death.

forensics
The study of physical evidence such as bloodstains, fingerprints, threads, and hair that helps investigators solve a crime.

grand jury
A group of citizens tasked with examining accusations to determine whether criminal charges should be filed.

hippie
A person who rejects conventional society, usually young and living in communal spaces, specifically during the late 1960s and 1970s.

homicide
When one person kills another person.

jurisdiction
A certain area within which a group has authority to make a legal decision or take legal action.

larceny
The theft of personal property.

occult
Related to secretive and often magical practices.

parole
Early release from prison because of good behavior under the condition that good behavior continue.

polygraph
A device designed for detecting the truthfulness of statements made by a witness.

Prohibition
An era of the 1920s and early 1930s in which the United States banned the sale or manufacture of liquor.

reformatory
An institution for juvenile criminal offenders.

Scientology
A cultlike religious doctrine founded by science fiction author L. Ron Hubbard.

sentencing
The part of a criminal trial that determines the punishment of a guilty defendant.

testimony
Statements made by witnesses during an investigation or under oath in a courtroom.

verdict
The decision in a court case rendered by either a jury or judge.

ADDITIONAL RESOURCES

SELECTED BIBLIOGRAPHY

Bugliosi, Vincent, with Curt Gentry. *Helter Skelter: The True Story of the Manson Murders*. Norton, 2001.

King, Greg. *Sharon Tate and the Manson Murders*. Barricade, 2000.

Lake, Dianne. *Member of the Family: My Story of Charles Manson, Life Inside the Cult, and the Darkness That Ended the Sixties*. HarperCollins, 2017.

Wiehl, Lis W. *Hunting Charles Manson: The Quest for Justice in the Days of Helter Skelter*. Thomas Nelson, 2018.

FURTHER READINGS

Burling, Alexis. *The Son of Sam Killings*. Abdo, 2020.

Carmichael, L. E. *Forensic Science: In Pursuit of Justice*. Abdo, 2015.

Zullo, Allan. *Crime Scene Investigators*. Scholastic, 2015.

ONLINE RESOURCES

To learn more about the Manson Family murders, please visit **abdobooklinks.com** or scan this QR code. These links are routinely monitored and updated to provide the most current information available.

MORE INFORMATION

For more information on this subject, contact or visit the following organizations:

CRIME VICTIMS ACTION ALLIANCE

1809 S St., Suite 101316
Sacramento, CA 95811
916-273-3603
cvactionalliance.com

Started as the Doris Tate Crime Victims Bureau, this group seeks to give victims a stronger voice in state legislatures and support new victims' rights laws.

DEARLY DEPARTED TOURS AND MUSEUM

5901 Santa Monica Blvd.
Los Angeles, CA 90038
855-600-3323
dearlydepartedtours.com

For the morbidly curious, this company offers guided tours to the dark side of Hollywood, including famous murder scenes. The Manson tour is one of its most popular.

SOURCE NOTES

CHAPTER 1. MURDER ON CIELO DRIVE

1. Greg King. *Sharon Tate and the Manson Murders*. Barricade, 2000. 214–215.

2. Vincent Bugliosi with Curt Gentry. *Helter Skelter: The True Story of the Manson Murders*. Norton, 2001. 6.

3. Glenn McEntyre. "Lancaster Man the Lone Survivor of Manson Killings." *10TV News*, 20 Nov. 2017, 10tv.com. Accessed 22 July 2019.

4. Dial Torgerson. "Sharon Tate, Four Others Murdered," *Los Angeles Times*, 10 Aug. 1969, newspapers.com. Accessed 22 July 2019.

5. Bugliosi and Gentry, *Helter Skelter: The True Story of the Manson Murders*, 11.

6. Alisa Statman with Brie Tate. *Restless Souls*. HarperCollins, 2012. 56–57.

CHAPTER 2. TWO HOMICIDE CASES

1. Vincent Bugliosi with Curt Gentry. *Helter Skelter: The True Story of the Manson Murders*. Norton, 2001. 42.

2. Greg King. *Sharon Tate and the Manson Murders*. Barricade, 2000. 243.

3. Bugliosi and Gentry, *Helter Skelter: The True Story of the Manson Murders*, 59.

4. Bugliosi and Gentry, *Helter Skelter: The True Story of the Manson Murders*, 61.

5. King, *Sharon Tate and the Manson Murders*, 235.

CHAPTER 3. CHARLES MANSON

1. Charles Manson with Nuel Emmons. *Manson in His Own Words*. Grove, 1986. Excerpted at *Grove Atlantic*, groveatlantic.com. Accessed 22 July 2019.

2. Vincent Bugliosi with Curt Gentry. *Helter Skelter: The True Story of the Manson Murders*. Norton, 2001. 144.

3. Julie Thompson. *The Hunt for the Last Public Enemy in Northeastern Ohio: Alvin "Creepy" Karpis and His Road to Alcatraz*. History, 2019. 159.

CHAPTER 4. TURNING TO MURDER

1. Dianne Lake. *Member of the Family*. William Morrow, 2017. 124–125.

2. "Danny DeCarlo Hinman Statement." *RXSTR.com*, n.d, rxstr.com. Accessed 22 July 2019.

3. Revelation 9:15. *King James Version*. *Bible Hub*, n.d, biblehub.com. Access 22 July 2019.

4. "McCartney Interview: Promoting the White Album 11/20/1968." *Beatles Interview Database*, n.d, beatlesinterviews.org. Accessed 22 July 2019.

5. Vincent Bugliosi with Curt Gentry. *Helter Skelter: The True Story of the Manson Murders*. Norton, 2001. 318.

SOURCE NOTES CONTINUED

CHAPTER 5. HELTER SKELTER

1. Alisa Statman with Brie Tate. *Restless Souls*. HarperCollins, 2012. 72.

CHAPTER 6. CLOSING IN ON THE FAMILY

1. Kelly Wynne. "Where Are Charles Manson's 'Family Members' Now?" *Newsweek*, 5 Apr. 2019, newsweek.com. Accessed 29 July 2019.

2. Bobby Beausoleil. *Voodoo Shivaya*. Light in the Attic Records, 2015, lightintheattic.net. Accessed 22 July 2019.

CHAPTER 7. MAKING THE CASE

1. Gerald and Kathleen Hill. "Beyond a Reasonable Doubt." *People's Law Dictionary*. Law.com, n.d, dictionary.law.com. Accessed 22 July 2019.

2. Vincent Bugliosi with Curt Gentry. *Helter Skelter: The True Story of the Manson Murders*. Norton, 2001. 263.

3. Los Angeles, California, Grand Jury. "Testimony of Susan Atkins." CieloDrive.com, 5 Dec. 1969, cielodrive.com. Accessed 22 July 2019.

4. Bugliosi and Gentry, *Helter Skelter: The True Story of the Manson Murders*, 263.

CHAPTER 8. THE TRIAL

1. California Court of Appeals. *People v. Manson. Justia.com*, n.d, law.justia.com. Accessed 22 July 2019.

2. Ben Beaumont-Thomas. "Julian Wasser's Best Shot: Roman Polanski at the Scene of the Manson Family Killings." *Guardian*, 10 July 2014, theguardian.com. Accessed 22 July 2019.

3. Samuel Osborne. "Charles Manson: Who Was the Infamous Cult Leader and What Did He Do?" *Independent*, 20 Nov. 2017, independent.co.uk. Access 22 July 2019.

4. United Press International. "Manson Displays to Jurors Headline of Nixon Remark." *New York Times*, 5 Aug. 1970, nytimes.com. Accessed 22 July 2019.

5. Vincent Bugliosi with Curt Gentry. *Helter Skelter: The True Story of the Manson Murders*. Norton, 2001. 379.

6. Lis Wiehl. *Hunting Charles Manson: The Quest for Justice in the Days of Helter Skelter*. Nelson, 2018. 209.

7. Bugliosi and Gentry, *Helter Skelter: The True Story of the Manson Murders*, 503.

8. Wiehl, *Hunting Charles Manson: The Quest for Justice in the Days of Helter Skelter*, 206.

9. Wiehl, *Hunting Charles Manson: The Quest for Justice in the Days of Helter Skelter*, 206.

CHAPTER 9. THE VERDICTS

1. Matt Hamilton. "Manson Follower Leslie Van Houten Granted Parole in Notorious Murders; LaBianca Family Opposes Her Release." *Los Angeles Times*, 7 Sept. 2017, latimes.com. Accessed 22 July 2019.

2. Hamilton, "Manson Follower Leslie Van Houten Granted Parole."

3. Vincent Bugliosi with Curt Gentry. *Helter Skelter: The True Story of the Manson Murders*. Norton, 2001. 230.

4. Christina Ng. "The Business of 'Murderabilia': Websites Selling Murder Memorabilia." *ABC News*, 7 Nov. 2011, abcnews.go.com. Accessed 22 July 2019.

INDEX

Altobelli, Rudi, 8, 13, 18, 23, 95
Anger, Kenneth, 42
arson, 67–69
Asin, Ray, 7–8
Atkins, Susan "Sadie," 44–45, 50, 52–55, 65–66, 69, 70–76, 78, 80, 83, 88, 93–94

Barker Ranch, 65, 67, 69, 75
Beach Boys, The, 39, 42
Beatles, The, 35, 39, 49, 84
   "Blackbird," 50
   McCartney, Paul, 49
   "Piggies," 50
   "Revolution 9," 51
   "Rocky Raccoon," 50
   "Sexy Sadie," 50
   White Album, The, 49
Beatty, Warren, 25
Beausoleil, Bobby, 42–46, 58, 65, 69
Beausoleil, Gail, 68–69
Bergen, Candice, 6, 42
Black Panthers, 45
Bonanza, 36
Book of Revelation, 48–49
Brunner, Mary, 33, 35, 44–45
Bugliosi, Vincent, 51, 73–75, 77–79, 84–86, 95–96

Chapman, Winifred, 4–9, 14
consumerism, 33, 40
counterculture, 39, 60, 82, 97
Crowe, Bernard "Lotsapoppa," 45

Davis, Bruce, 44
Day, Doris, 44
death penalty, 75, 88, 92–94
Death Valley, 65–66, 76
DeCarlo, Danny, 73
DeRosa, Jerry, 7, 9, 12–13
Dorgan, Joe, 16
drugs, 18, 20, 22–23, 33, 40, 43, 45, 58–59, 60, 84
Duel in the Sun, 36

Folger, Abigail, 8–9, 11, 13, 19, 54, 79
Folger, Peter, 8
forensics, 12, 55
Fromme, Lynette "Squeaky," 35
Frykowski, Voytek, 9, 11, 19, 54, 79

Galindo, Danny, 16
Garretson, William, 9–10, 18–20, 57
Gleason, William, 28
Graham, Virginia, 70, 72–73
Granado, Joe, 12
Grogan, Steve, 54–55, 64

Haight-Ashbury, 32–35, 42, 93
Helter Skelter, 16, 39, 45, 48–49, 51, 65, 67, 75, 78, 84, 94–95
Hinman, Gary, 43–48, 58, 62, 66, 69
hippies, 35, 39, 42, 60
Howard, Ronnie, 72
Hoyt, Barbara, 83–84
Hughes, Ronald, 88

Kanarek, Irving, 80, 90
Karpis, Alvin "Creepy," 31
Kasabian, Linda, 52, 54–55, 66, 75–79, 90
Keith, Maxwell, 92
Krenwinkel, Patricia, 35, 52–55, 75–78, 80, 88, 93

LaBianca, Leno, 14–17
LaBianca, Rosemary, 14–16, 54
LaBianca murders, 16–19, 23, 24, 42, 54–55, 58–59, 62, 65, 70, 73–75, 78, 82, 90, 93
Lake, Dianne, 41
Lee, William, 57
Lomax, Ed, 57
Lone Ranger, The, 36
Los Angeles Police Department (LAPD), 12–13, 17, 23, 57, 60–61
Los Angeles Times, 10, 61
Lutesinger, Kitty, 66

Maddox, Kathleen, 30
Manson, Charles, 28–35, 38–51, 52–55, 62–69, 70, 73–79, 80–86, 88–89, 90–97
Manson, William, 30
McCauley, K. J., 23
Melcher, Terry, 42, 95
murder weapons
 gun, 44, 54, 57–61, 72–73, 77, 79
 knife, 9, 23, 45–46, 54, 57
Myers Ranch, 65, 69

Nader, Saladin, 55
Newsweek, 20
Nixon, Richard, 83
Noguchi, Thomas, 12

Older, Charles, 80, 82–82, 86, 88, 92
10050 Cielo Drive, 4, 7, 10–13, 14, 17, 20, 22, 23, 42, 52, 55, 59, 70, 76, 78–79, 82, 94–96

Parent, Steve, 10, 11, 54, 72, 79
parole, 28, 31, 64, 93, 94, 95
Polanski, Roman, 7, 8, 9, 18, 20–22, 25, 59, 82
Powell, Richard, 67–68

satanic rituals, 12, 18, 20, 22, 59
Schram, Stephanie, 66
Scientology, 33
Sebring, Jay, 8–9, 11, 54, 57, 70, 73
Sellers, Peter, 25
Shea, Donald "Shorty," 64–65, 73, 83
Shinn, Dave, 83
Spahn, George, 26, 36–38, 64
Spahn Movie Ranch, 26, 28, 36, 39, 42–44, 45, 46, 48, 55, 62, 64–66, 67, 73, 75, 79, 84
Straight Satans, 43, 73
Struthers, Frank, 14–16
Struthers, Suzan, 16
Summer of Love, 32–33

Tate, Debra, 22, 94
Tate, Doris, 94
Tate, Paul "PJ," 22, 60

Tate, Sharon, 7–8, 9, 10, 11, 12, 13, 20, 22, 23, 25, 54–57, 59, 60, 61, 65, 70, 78, 83, 94
Tate murders, 16–18, 23–24, 26, 42, 55–61, 62, 70, 72–75, 78, 82–83, 90, 93
Torgerson, Dial, 10

Van Houten, Leslie, 54–55, 65, 75–76, 80, 88, 92–93
victim impact statements, 94
Victims' Bill of Rights, 94

Watkins, Paul, 51, 84–86
Watson, Tex, 45, 52–54, 64, 66, 70, 75–79, 93
Weiss, Bernard, 60, 72
Weiss, Steven, 59–61, 72
Whisenhunt, William, 9
Wilson, Dennis, 39, 42

ABOUT THE AUTHOR

Tom Streissguth has written more than 100 books of nonfiction, including works of history, geography, biography, and current events, for the school and library market. He has also created a website dedicated to the little-known works of writers such as Ernest Hemingway, Jack London, Nellie Bly, Stephen Crane, and H. L. Mencken. He lives in Saint Paul, Minnesota, and has a second home in Thailand.